D1413510

Jan 2007

Ceidi

To my coffee buddy . . .

a passion for
coffee

heres to many more grandes!

Love
Heidi

a passion for
coffee

hattie ellis

photography by debi treloar

RYLAND
PETERS
& SMALL
LONDON NEW YORK

Designer Jo Fernandes
Senior Editor Clare Double
Picture Research Emily Westlake
Production Eleanor Cant
Art Director Anne-Marie Bulat
Publishing Director Alison Starling
Stylist Emily Chalmers
Food Stylist Fiona Smith

First published in the United States in 2006
by Ryland Peters & Small
519 Broadway, 5th Floor
New York, NY 10012
www.rylandpeters.com

10 9 8 7 6 5 4 3 2
Text, design, and commissioned photographs
© Ryland Peters & Small 2002, 2006
A longer version of this text was previously
published in *Coffee* (2002).

ISBN-10: 1-84597-230-9
ISBN-13: 978-1-84597-230-1
Printed and bound in China

contents

Coffea arabica

what is coffee?

Coffee beans begin life as the seeds inside the cherries of an evergreen plant, *Coffea arabica*, which grows in the humid lands between the tropic of Cancer and the tropic of Capricorn. They range from fruity Kenyans to chocolatey Guatemalans, from spicy Indonesians to clean Costa Ricans.

After the cherries are harvested, their outer layers are removed and the green beans found within travel around the globe. Roasted, ground, and mixed with hot water, the beans' concentrated, aromatic flavors are released to make one of the most remarkable and celebrated drinks in the world. Transformed

from plant to cup, the tastes—of lemon, of blueberries, of wine—that lie within this bitter black brew can still remind you of its origins at the heart of a fruit.

Ancient as tribes and irrepressibly modern, coffee adapts itself to time and place, encompassing the romantic, the industrious, and the day-to-day. Its dynamic history is full of tales of passion and intrigue, yet it is also the everyday drink of breakfast and of mid-morning office breaks. Prized for its intriguing range of flavors and styles, used as a digestive, and relied upon as a stimulant, coffee excites and focuses the brain along with the rest of the body. It brings us

together over cups and conversation. Its aromatic allure can beckon us away from our daily business to a café for a quiet sip, a newspaper, and a view of the world. Solitary or sociable, it allows us both to unwind and to recharge.

The current surge of interest in coffee has developed through a growing awareness of the quality end of the market, in freshly roasted beans that have a particular provenance and a distinctive taste, and in the many ways of drinking coffee, such as cappuccino and espresso. A *Passion for Coffee* celebrates coffee in all its forms and looks at how to discover and enjoy its many flavors.

the buzz

the origins of coffee

Ethiopia, believed by many to be the ancient birthplace of mankind, is where coffee's long history begins. Legend tells of Kaldi, a goatherd in Abyssinia who noticed his animals prancing around after nibbling at the leaves and fruit of particular bushes. So, right from the start, the plant was recognized and prized as a stimulant. Monks took coffee to keep them awake for nocturnal prayers, and travelers rolled the cherries with fat into balls to make an early trail food.

Coffea arabica was cultivated by the Arabs, who used coffee both as a medicine and as a pleasurable stimulant.

Coffeehouses sprang up where people would meet to drink, play backgammon, talk, and listen to music and storytelling. Pilgrims and traders spread the bean around the Muslim world, and its fame— and consumption—spanned North Africa, Turkey, and Persia.

Coffeehouses came to be regarded as subversive—as places of temptation and ideological ferment—but the drink's progress around the world was indefatigable, as people discovered this *qahwa al-bon*, "wine of the bean," that could waken mind, spirit, and senses.

spread around the world

Coffee consumption took off in the West in the 17th century. One of the bean's early European destinations was the trade center of Venice, which received coffee with other goods from the East. At first, Christian leaders rejected the drink as darkly satanic. However, once Pope Clement VIII took a sip, he blessed the new brew as heavenly instead.

Coffeehouses popularized the drink wherever it was consumed. Coinciding with the founding of newspapers and the thinking of the Enlightenment, coffee became known as the drink of democracy. British coffeehouses were called "penny universities" because, for the price of a cup, people could meet and discuss politics and philosophy.

The first French café, Café Procope, opened its doors opposite the Comédie Française in 1689, and soon became the haunt of philosophers, writers, and political activists. By the end of the 18th century there were 800 cafés in Paris, and by 1843 there were 3,000.

After the Boston Tea Party, Americans saw tea as unpatriotic and became a nation of coffee drinkers. The bean, now grown outside Africa and Arabia, arrived on the doorstep of the booming U.S. market in Latin America, which was to become the world's biggest producer of coffee.

coffee trade

Coffee grows on vast Brazilian plantations and is collected from the wild in Ethiopian forests; it is cultivated on ancient terraces carved into the mountainsides of Yemen and on Indonesian smallholdings. In volume, coffee is the second most traded commodity in the world, after oil.

Coffee production can be affected by political upheaval, when growers may switch from export crops to subsistence farming, and it is prone to the natural disasters, such as hurricanes and floods, that can devastate the tropics. Global price fluctuations can mean bankruptcy to

the small grower, which is why the Fair Trade movement (see page 63) guarantees a stable price that goes directly to the producer and enables them to continue farming in a sustainable way.

Some of the best coffees end up in specialized coffee suppliers. They have the experience and contacts to source consistently good beans from the market, tasting each new crop and roasting every batch of beans to perfection to bring out their optimum flavors. To find them, just follow the tantalizing aromas that wisp out from a good coffee shop or café.

famous coffee drinkers

Coffee gives people energy, and cafés bring them together—a potent combination. Voltaire downed as many as 50 cups a day. Beethoven would count 60 beans into a single cup. Balzac walked across Paris to get three kinds of coffee from different shops to make a blend that kept him awake to write from midnight until midday. He explained that when he drank coffee, "... ideas begin to move ... the paper is covered in ink."

The Boston Tea Party was planned in secrecy at the Green Dragon coffeehouse. And, just a few years later in 1789, Desmoulins whipped up a revolutionary crowd when he leapt onto a table to speak from the Café Foy in Paris; two days later, the Bastille was stormed.

"Strong coffee, and plenty, awakens me," said Napoleon, who favored a Brazilian Santos-Mocha blend. "It gives me warmth, an unusual force, a pain that is not without pleasure."

Jean-Paul Sartre and Simone de Beauvoir wrote at Les Deux Magots, a Left Bank café, while the Beat Poets drank coffee and talked the talk at the Caffe Trieste and the Co-Existence Bagel Shop in San Francisco. Impressionism, Surrealism, Cubism, Existentialism—all these movements were brewed in the atmosphere of cafés and coffee shops.

the beans

understanding terms

Arabica beans, from *Coffea arabica*, are the coffee connoisseur's choice. The plant grows best at higher altitudes, and its slowly grown, hard beans have more flavor than coffees from the more easily grown *Coffea robusta* beans. Look also for coffee labeled "high grown" or "hard bean."

Older varieties of the arabica coffee plant, such as Bourbon, are worth seeking out. So, too, are specialties such as Peaberry coffee, which comes from cherries with a single, rounder bean, and the large Maragogype, or "elephant" beans, which are prized both for their appearance and their smooth taste.

The way in which the beans are separated from their surrounding pulp also plays a part in the character of the coffee in your cup. Wet-processed, or washed, beans tend to have lighter, subtle flavors, while the dry-processed beans, from areas where water is in short supply, can have an earthy, fruity character.

When tasting coffee, notice the aroma and the flavors inside the cup; the body, which is the feel of the coffee in your mouth, cleanly light to lusciously full; and its acidity, which spreads across your tongue and lifts the drink by providing an additional, lively layer of enjoyment.

roasts and blends

Coffee is exported as green beans.
These are sent around the world in
sacks, and are then roasted by specialists
to bring out their subtle flavors. As the
beans heat up and turn a glossy brown,
the oils that are the secret of their
marvelous flavor develop.

Roasts vary from light brown
through medium to the very dark beans
favoured by the French and Italians.
Light roasts, such as "cinnamon," have
a more delicate, mildly aromatic taste.
Medium roasts, also known as "city"
or "American," are slightly stronger.
Viennese roasts are a little darker still
than medium, while French, Italian,
and Continental roasts edge into deep
brown and near-black, producing

enticingly bitter, richly pungent flavors, such as those found in espresso.

The art of blending is to marry different beans together to create a harmonious balance of flavors, acidity, and body. Specialized coffee suppliers pride themselves on their variations on classics, such as mellow breakfast blends, stronger after-dinner blends, and those used to make espresso. One long-standing combination is Mocha-Java, which combines aroma and strength to make a delicious, potent brew. It takes skill and constant tasting to create and maintain house blends, as even beans from the same place will vary from batch to batch and from year to year.

the Americas

Since the plant was first cultivated commercially on the continent in the 18th century, the Americas have become the largest producers of coffee in the world. Costa Rican beans are highly prized for their fragrance, balance, and entrancing acidity. Tarrazu is the most famous region in a land known as the Switzerland of coffee countries for its consistency, clean flavors, and attention to detail. This is a good place to source high-altitude beans, such as the high-grade Strictly Hard Bean (SHB).

For a contrast in style, the rugged terrain and remote highlands of Guatemala produce smoky, chocolatey, fruity beans loved for their distinctive individuality. Look out for beans such as those from Huehuetenango, the volcanic slopes above the city of Antigua, and the moist climate of Cobán.

Brazil grows around a third of the world's coffee, much of it on vast plantations. Specialists hunt out high-grade Brazilian coffees, such as those from the older Bourbon plant. Colombia, the second largest coffee producer in the world, is known for the full-bodied, mellow consistency of its washed coffees, from the *supremo* (large) to *excelso* (smaller) beans.

Mexico produces nutty beans with Central American acidity, and is known for its extra-large Maragogype beans. Hawaii has the smooth, complex Kona coffees, and Jamaica's Blue Mountain is famous for its high-quality beans, which command equally high prices.

Africa

Some coffee grows wild in its indigenous home of Ethiopia, and the beans produced from this ancient land intrigue drinkers with their winey, gamey, perfumed flavors and aromatic hints of apricots, blueberries, lemon, grapes, and flowers. Look out for coffees such as those from Harrar and from the Sidamo region, which may be labeled after the town of Yirgacheffe. Likely to be grown without pesticides or artificial fertilizers, the natural wildness of these plants translates into the cup as rare, interesting coffees.

Across the Red Sea, Yemeni coffees share some of the same characteristics and may be called Mocha, after the port that exported early coffees to Europe. These beans of Arabia can be perfumed with a heavy-bodied piquancy and a bright acidity. Dry-processed, they can be earthy with an almost liquorice tang. Mattari and Sanani coffees are the best known.

Grown high up, some at over 5,000 feet, Kenyan coffees can stop you in your tracks with their pure, fresh, tangy tastes. Kenyan beans are loved for their balance of beautiful body, clean acidity, and berry fruitiness. The top-grade beans are graded AA, and are wet-processed. Kenyan Peaberries, with their single fruit, are a specialty and have a satisfyingly rounded appearance and a smooth, sometimes malty, taste.

Tanzania, Zimbabwe, and Malawi can all grow coffee with the sparkling acidity and fruitiness of the East African style.

Asia

The Dutch first grew coffee on the Indonesian island of Java, and its name has been used to refer to all the coffees from this country and, historically, for coffee in general. Javanese coffees are known for their earthy, spicy, rich flavors. Sumatra and Sulawesi also grow luscious, full-bodied coffees with strong, distinctive flavors of herbs, woods, spices, and even syrupy-smooth caramel. Sulawesi coffees are sometimes sold under the former Dutch name for the island, Celebes.

One intriguing, and expensive, Indonesian specialty is the Kopi Luak coffee, made from beans eaten and excreted by a small, catlike wild animal, the luak. The beans, transformed in the animal's digestive tract, have, as you might imagine, something of a cult following. Some Indonesian coffees are aged to mimic the taste acquired when the beans were stockpiled in the islands' damp, warm climate or underwent long sea voyages to the West. Neighboring Papua New Guinea produces coffees with a perfumed tropical fruitiness.

Coffee has been grown in India since the 17th century and specialties include aged Monsoon coffees, where the beans are exposed to the monsoon winds in open warehouses. The result is a coffee with a special, mellow flavor. Southern India grows coffees with enticing scents of spices. Mysore coffees are one kind known for quality, as they come from a state where arabica plants are grown.

flavored coffee

Certain flavors have an affinity with coffee, hence the chocolate on the top of a cappuccino or the spoonful of vanilla sugar added to an after-dinner cup. Spiced coffees are traditional in the Middle East, where the grounds may be mixed with cardamom and other flavors such as nutmeg, cinnamon, and cloves. On parts of the Amalfi coast in Italy, they sometimes add a twist of peel from their famous lemons, and the habit has followed some Italians living in America. Modern flavored coffees use essential oils to make such brews as pecan and raspberries and cream. You can also buy or make flavored sugar syrups to add to brewed coffees (orange is a good one), or add a dash of a liqueur for a tasty kick.

decaffeinated coffee

Decaffeinated coffees are made by dissolving the caffeine out of the beans using chemical solvents or water. Look for decaf sold by people who care about quality. Some of the taste disappears with the caffeine, so the coffee must be made from beans with plenty of flavor in the first place. Lesser suppliers use cheap, less delicious beans to compensate for the cost of the decaffeination process, which is why the drink can taste underpowered in more than one sense. Robusta coffees, incidentally, contain about twice as much caffeine as the higher-quality arabicas.

the brew

buying and storing

Coffee becomes much more interesting if you buy it from a specialized supplier. You can purchase through the internet and by mail order, or steep yourself in the sensory delight of the store itself with all its aromas and busy sounds: the grinding, the chinking, the shake, rattle, and roll of the beans. A good retailer will have a wide choice of high-quality beans; they may do their own roasting, and will be able to give you advice on what to try.

Freshness is the key to good coffee. The aromatic oils start to disappear immediately after roasting, so it is best to buy small amounts of freshly roasted beans regularly, instead of a large amount in one trip. Buy coffee as you would other fresh foods, and use it at its peak. When beans are freshly roasted, the grounds tend to foam up when you add water.

For best results, buy whole beans and grind them at home just before brewing, because the oils lose their volatile aromas even more quickly once the coffee is ground. A good retailer will also grind beans for you. An inexpensive propeller-blade grinder is a good way to start, or pay more for a grinder that mills the coffee between disks to get a more even grind and has settings that can be adjusted for different grades, from coarse to fine.

Coffee should be stored in an airtight, dry container, in a cool cabinet rather than the refrigerator. You can also freeze beans in an airtight bag for a couple of months, and grind them while still frozen.

secrets of the perfect cup

These four principles make all the difference between insipid meekness or brutish bitterness and what you want in coffee—aromatic energy.

• Buy freshly roasted, good-quality beans and grind just before brewing.

• Make sure the grind is right for the method you are using.

• Measure the coffee and water you need and the brewing time. Getting the correct proportion of coffee to water and letting them brew together for the right amount of time means you extract maximum character and aromatic oils from the beans without the brew becoming bitter. If you want weaker coffee, it is better to add hot water to properly brewed coffee than to use too much water or too few beans.

• With the exception of Middle Eastern coffee, which is boiled, pour the water onto the grounds when it has just boiled. This dissolves the soluble flavors from the coffee without scalding the subtleties into bitterness. Do not keep coffee warm on the heat or it will become bitter.

espresso know-how

Espresso is made by forcing hot water through finely ground, dark-roasted coffee under pressure so that it blasts through the grounds, extracting the maximum flavor.

At home, Italians often make espressos in a stove-top pot; the Moka is the classic model. Fill the bottom half with water up to the rivet on the side and fill the coffee container up to the brim with finely ground coffee, leveling it off gently so the water can get through evenly. Screw the top tightly onto the bottom. When the coffee is ready, you will hear air bubbling through the connecting tube, once all the water has gone through.

If you want to buy an espresso machine, go for one that provides high pressure, such as a pump-action model, to get most flavor. Expensive versions approach the engineering of those used in cafés. You can also buy machines with ready-to-use coffee pods, but this restricts your choice, and the beans are not freshly ground.

French presses and more

All these methods require 2 tablespoons coffee per ¾ cup (180 ml) water and need to brew for 4–6 minutes to extract the beans' fullest flavor.

• The popular plunge-pot, French press, or cafetière, uses coarsely ground coffee. Give the coffee a stir once you have poured on the water. Infuse for 4 minutes. You can wrap a dishtowel around the pot to keep the liquid hot while brewing, or use an insulated plunge-pot.

• When making filter coffee, wet the medium-fine ground coffee first with a little hot water to help the water filter through evenly.

• Old-fashioned French drip pots work on the same principle as filter coffee and come in three parts: a pot, a filter with holes, and a top section with a lid. You put medium ground coffee in the filter, pour water into the top part, and let it drip through to the bottom.

• Recently revived, the vacuum-pot method requires a medium-fine grind and produces coffee with a beautiful clarity of flavor.

milk and sugar?

Milk goes with coffee in many delicious ways. Hot milk works better than cold: French waiters will simultaneously pour a jet of coffee from one pot and hot milk from another to form a *café au lait*; an Italian "stains" an espresso with a drop of steamed milk to make *caffè macchiato* or adds it, half and half, to make a latte.

Milk softens and alters flavors. When trying a new bean, taste the coffee black first, then add milk and judge how its character is altered. Cream also adds a layer of smoothness to a cup.

Sugar takes away some of the bitterness in coffee, though well-made coffee should have only a subtle edge of bitterness. You may like to add a spoonful to dark-roasted coffee, such as espresso, but not to lighter styles. Eating little pastries or cookies with your coffee is, of course, an excellent way to sweeten the moment.

cappuccino, latte, and au lait...

The classic cappuccino is made using one third espresso, one third steamed milk, and one third foam. Espresso machines usually have a metal wand that steams and froths the milk. Alternatively, heat milk in a saucepan or microwave and then whisk it by hand until it froths. You can also buy electric milk-frothing whisks, some of which come with containers that go in the microwave to heat the milk. Pour the hot milk onto the coffee, holding back the froth with a spoon, and add the frothed milk last. If desired, top off the cappuccino with powdered chocolate.

You can also drink a *cappuccino senza schiuma* (without foam); a *cappuccino chiaro*, with less coffee and more milk; or the darker *cappuccino scuro*, which contains less milk. Just use your eye and your tastebuds to judge the proportions.

A *caffè latte* is made from roughly half hot or steamed milk and half espresso mixed together. The French *café au lait* is the same, except that it is made with filter coffee.

café society

There are many reasons for coffee's popularity, from the medical to the gastronomic, but at base its appeal is that the caffeine it contains is quickly absorbed into the bloodstream, providing a hit of mental alertness. Different countries have evolved places where people can drink and take a break, from the zinc-topped counters of French cafés and the wood-paneled sophistication of the Viennese coffeehouse to the bright zap of the modern coffee chain. Café society is about people meeting, thinking, writing, talking—or simply taking time out with a coffee brew.

Italian coffee drinking

Hot shots of coffee fuel the animated Italians. Cappuccino is a milky breakfast brew that may be drunk with a *cornetto* (croissant). The drink, with its hood of frothed milk, is named after the color of Capuchin monks' habits. The monks themselves were named after their own hoods (*cappuccio*).

The classic espresso is a very short measure— just a few long, deliciously bitter sips—and a well-made one has a pale brown foam, or *crema*, on top. A *caffè doppio* is a double measure. *Caffè lungo* has more water for a milder drink and *caffè ristretto* has less water for a stronger brew. A *caffè macchiato* contains a dollop of steamed milk, while a *latte macchiato* is milk with a drop of coffee.

On hot days, you can refresh yourself with a *caffè freddo* (iced coffee) or a *caffè latte freddo*, with milk. And on a cold day, or after dinner, you could add a drop of spirits for a fortifying *caffè corretto*.

Middle Eastern coffee

An *ibrik*, or *kanaka*, is the tapered pot with a long handle and a pouring lip used in the Middle Eastern method of boiling coffee with water. Mix one or two heaped teaspoons of very finely ground coffee with an equal amount of sugar for each demitasse (little cup) of water. The *ibrik* must be only half full, as the mixture will expand as it boils. Bring to a boil over medium heat, then reduce the heat to low. Bring to a boil again, then either turn the heat off, or repeat the boiling once more.

Half fill the cups with coffee, then add some of the prized foam to the top of each drink. For an extra-aromatic brew, use Middle Eastern coffee that is ready-mixed with cardamom.

spiced orange coffee syrup

10 green cardamom pods

1¼ cups (250 g) sugar

½ cup (125 ml) strong coffee or espresso

1 teaspoon finely grated orange zest

1 cinnamon stick, broken into pieces

serves 6–8

A syrup for ice cream spiced with the cardamom that often flavors Middle Eastern coffee.

Crush the cardamom pods with a knife and scrape out the seeds. Put the sugar into a heavy-bottomed saucepan, add ¼ cup (60 ml) water and heat very slowly until the sugar dissolves—gently draw a spoon across the sugar to help the process. When all the sugar has dissolved, boil for 2 minutes, then stir in the coffee, orange zest, cinnamon, and cardamom. Let it cool so the flavors infuse, then strain and store the syrup in an airtight container in the refrigerator.

To serve, pour onto vanilla or chocolate ice cream.

coffee and alcohol

Coffee is often served at the end of a meal and
it combines beautifully with liqueurs, enjoyed
either alongside one another, or in the same
cup. To make Irish coffee, pour Irish whiskey
(other liquor works well, too) into a glass with
a spoonful of sugar, add strong, hot coffee, and
pour heavy cream over the back of a spoon so it
floats on top. Alternatively, simply add a drop of
brandy, Calvados, grappa, or another liqueur
to black or white coffee for an extra glow of
heat. Rum and orange-flavored liqueurs
such as Cointreau work particularly well.

iced coffee

2 tablespoons ground coffee

4 ice cubes

1 small scoop vanilla or chocolate ice cream (optional)

½ cup (125 ml) milk

1 teaspoon sugar, or to taste

a dash of liqueur (optional)

serves 1

You can add a splash of a liqueur, such as Cointreau or rum, to this deliciously refreshing drink.

Brew the coffee using your regular method, but make it stronger than usual (using ½ cup (125 ml) water to the 2 tablespoons ground coffee) because it will be diluted by the ice. When brewed, pour the coffee onto the ice cubes. As an extra touch, you can put a small scoop of ice cream on the ice cubes before you pour in the coffee. Stir in the milk, sugar, and liqueur, if using.

Serve immediately or chill until required.

useful addresses

Allegro Coffee Company
12799 Claude Court
Building B, Dock 4
Thornton, CO 80241
(800) 666 4869
www.allegro-coffee.com

Ancora Coffee Roasters
3701 Orin Road
Madison, WI 53704
(800) 260 0217
www.ancora-coffee.com

Caffè Appassionato
4001 21st Avenue West
Seattle, WA 98199
(888) 502 2333
www.caffeappassionato.com

The Coffee Mill Roastery
161 East Franklin Street
Chapel Hill, NC 27514
(919) 929 1727

Daybreak Coffee Roasters
2377 Main Street
Glastonbury, CT 06033
(800) 882 5282
www.daybreakcoffee.com

**Distant Lands
Coffee Roaster**
11754 State Highway 64
West
Tyler, TX 75704-9493
(800) 346 5459
www.dlcoffee.com

Graffeo
735 Columbus Avenue
San Francisco, CA 94113
(800) 222 6250
www.graffeo.com

**Green Mountain
Coffee Roasters**
33 Coffee Lane
Waterbury, VT 05676
(888) 879 4627
www.GreenMountain
Coffee.com

**Greene Brothers Speciality
Coffee Roasters**
313 High Street
Hackettstown, NJ 07840
(908) 979 0022
www.greenesbeans.com

**H. R. Higgins
(Coffee-Man) Ltd**
79 Duke Street
London W1K 5AS, UK
+44 20 7629 3913
www.hrhiggins.co.uk

www.ineedcoffee.com

Layton Fern & Co. Ltd
27 Rathbone Place
London W1T 1EP, UK
+44 20 7636 2237
www.laytonfern.fsnet.co.uk

**McNulty's Tea and
Coffee Company**
109 Christopher Street
New York, NY 10014
(212) 242 5351
(800) 356-5200 to order
www.mcnultys.com

Monmouth Coffee Company
27 Monmouth Street
London WC2H 9DD, UK
+44 20 7379 3516
and

2 Park Street
London SE1 9AB, UK
+44 20 7645 3585
www.monmouth
    coffee.co.uk

**The Original San Juan
Coffee Roasting Company**
18 Cannery Landing
Friday Harbor, WA 98250
(800) 624 4119
www.rockisland.com
    /~sjcoffee/

Ozzie's Coffee and Tea
57 Seventh Avenue
Brooklyn, NY 11215
and
249 Fifth Avenue
Brooklyn, NY 11215
(888) 699 4371
www.ozziescoffee.com

Peaberry Coffee
1299 East 58th Avenue
Denver, CO 80216
(303) 292 9324
www.peaberrycoffee.com

Peet's Coffee and Tea
PO Box 12509
Berkeley, CA 94712-3509
(800) 999 2132
www.peets.com

Royal Blend
601 NE First Street
Bend, OR 97701
(800) 742 2690
www.royalblend.com

Urth Caffé
8565 Melrose Avenue
West Hollywood,
CA 90069
(310) 659 0628
www.urthcaffe.com

Fair Trade organizations

The Fair Trade principle
is a commitment to
setting new standards
for commercial trading
in developing countries.

Equal Exchange
50 United Drive
West Bridgewater,
MA 02379
(774) 776 7400
www.equalexchange.com

Cafédirect
City Cloisters, Suite B2
196 Old Street
London EC1V 9FR, UK
+44 20 7490 9520
www.cafedirect.co.uk

TransFair USA
1611 Telegraph Avenue,
Suite 900
Oakland, CA 94612
(510) 663 5260
www.transfairusa.org

To Clare Moberly

picture credits

All photographs by Debi Treloar except the following:

William Lingwood
Pages 56, 57, 59

James Merrell
Pages 34, 38 below right, 55

David Brittain
Page 3

Peter Cassidy
Page 54

Christopher Drake
Page 51 right

Diana Miller
Page 2

Ian Wallace
Page 33

Polly Wreford
Pages 4–5

Francesca Yorke
Endpapers

PUBLISHER'S ACKNOWLEDGMENTS
The publisher would like to thank the
Monmouth Coffee Company, H. R. Higgins
(Coffee-Man) Ltd, and Layton Fern & Co. Ltd
for allowing us to photograph in their premises.